This belongs to

____

A **Shih Tzu** is a dog so fine,
With a coat of hair that's quite divine,
Big round eyes that sparkle and shine,
And a friendly personality that's simply divine.

A **Labrador Retriever** is a wonderful friend,
With a wagging tail that never ends,
Their coats are shiny and always smooth,
Their hearts are big, full of love to soothe.

The **Australian Shepherd** is a dog so bright,
Eyes of blue or brown, they're quite a sight,
With energy to spare, they're always in flight,
A fun companion, day or night.

A **Vizsla** with coat so rust,
Moves with agility and robust.
With eyes so kind and soulful stare,
This breed is loyal beyond compare.

The **Miniature Schnauzer** is a breed quite rare,
With bushy eyebrows and a beard to spare,
Intelligent and loyal, with a playful air,
A little dog with a big personality to share.

The **Pembroke Welsh Corgi** is a dog so sweet,
Short and stout with little feet,
A cheerful disposition that can't be beat,
A furry friend you'd always want to meet.

The **Great Dane** is a dog quite tall,
A gentle giant that will enthrall,
With a regal presence that stands above all,
A best friend who will answer your call.

With curly fur as white as snow,
A **Bichon Frise** is quite the show,
Friendly and happy, with a wag of the tail,
Their playful nature will never fail.

The **Chihuahua** is a tiny breed,
Small in size, but full of speed,
With a sassy attitude and a loyal creed,
A pint-sized pup that's sure to succeed.

With floppy ears and big brown eyes,
A **Cavalier King Charles Spaniel** lies.
Soft fur in shades of ruby and black,
A trustworthy companion, always has your back.

With tuxedo coat and pointy ears,
The **Boston Terrier** always appears,
Full of energy and playful fun,
A loyal friend to everyone.

With tri-colored fur and a gentle face,
The **Bernese Mountain Dog** exudes grace.
A dependable and devoted friend indeed,
Always there in times of need.

With fur as white as snow,
A **Maltese** is a charming show,
Small in size, but big in heart,
Their loyalty sets them apart.

A **Border Collie**, agile and bright,
With fur that's black and white.
A herding dog with endless might,
Ready to work both day and night.

With silver coat shining bright,
A **Weimaraner** cuts a striking sight.
With sleek lines and noble grace,
This breed steals hearts at a rapid pace.

The **French Bulldog**, with its bat-like ears,
An unwavering friend, that will calm your fears,
With a compact body and a happy face,
A roommate , that will fill your space.

A **West Highland White Terrier**, fluffy and fair,
With bright eyes and perky ears, always aware.
Small but mighty, a terrier through and through,
This breed's fun nature shines in all they do.

A **Shetland Sheepdog**, small and bright,
With thick coat and bark so light.
Quick and nimble, a herding pro,
This breed's intelligence steals the show.

With a sturdy frame and muscles so tight,
A **Staffordshire Bull Terrier** stands proud and right,
Smart and loving, with a heart of gold,
A true companion, never to fold.

With floppy ears and a wagging tail,
The **English Springer Spaniel** will never fail
To charm you with their playful ways,
They'll brighten up even the gloomiest of days.

A **Scottish Terrier** with coat so wiry,
Short legs and a tail that's fiery,
Brave and loyal, with heart so true,
A pint-sized pup with a big bark too!

A **Newfoundland**, so big and grand,
A gentle giant, with a paw like a hand,
A great friend, both loving and true,
With a heart as vast as the ocean blue.

American Staffordshire Terrier, muscles so defined,
Loyal and loving, with a heart refined,
A protector, with courage to spare,
A loyal friend, beyond compare.

A **Rhodesian Ridgeback**, a breed so fine,
Its coat with a ridge like a line,
A trustworthy friend, and oh so brave,
Always ready, to protect and save.

A **Beagle** with its nose to the ground,
In search of a scent that must be found,
With floppy ears and big brown eyes,
A great friend, with a heart full of surprise

The **Boxer** with its strong and agile frame,
A fun friend, that's always game,
With a playful bark and a joyful leap,
A playmate that's sure to keep.

An **Old English Sheepdog**, so furry and grand,
With a coat of fluff that covers the land.
A friendly giant, with a heart full of cheer,
A loyal companion, always near and dear.

The **Dachshund** with its body long and low,
A fearless pup, with a big brave glow,
With ears that flap and a nose that's keen,
A devoted friend, a sight to be seen.

The **Bulldog**, with its wrinkled face,
A staunch friend, with unbreakable grace,
With a sturdy build and a bark so deep,
A caring ally, that's yours to keep.

The **Doberman Pinscher**, sleek and strong,
A strong friend, that will never do you wrong,
With a coat so shiny, and a heart so pure,
A protector, that will always endure.

The **German Shepherd**, strong and bold,
A trusty partner, with a heart of gold,
With a powerful bark and a watchful eye,
A protector, that will never lie.

With fur as gold as the sun,
A **Golden Retriever**'s full of fun,
Dutiful, loving, and always a friend,
Their playful spirit will never end.

With a muscular build, they stand tall,
Rottweilers are strong and never small,
Loyal and brave, they guard with might,
Protecting their loved ones day and night.

A **Poodle**'s coat is curly and plush,
They're elegant and never rush,
With intelligence that can't be beat,
They make a fantastic friend, oh so sweet.

With eyes as blue as winter skies,
A **Siberian Husky**'s full of surprise,
Athletic, smart, and built for the snow,
Their friendship and devotion always show.

Small in size but big in heart,
Yorkshire Terriers are quite the work of art,
With glossy hair that's silky and fine,
Their charm and spunk will always shine.

A **Saint Bernard,** with a heart so true,
A gentle giant, always there for you,
With a massive head and a warm embrace,
In times of need, it's a comforting face.

The **English Cocker Spaniel**, so merry and bright,
With long silky ears, oh what a sight,
A faithful companion, with a wag in its tail,
A loving nature, that will never fail.

A **pug** is a dog that's quite small,
But don't let its size fool you at all,
With its squishy little face and curly tail,
A love for you will always prevail.

With a beautiful coat and a heart of gold,
A **Giant Schnauzer** is a sight to behold,
Loyal and brave, they stand tall and strong,
Protecting their family all day long.

With a muscular build and a charming grin,
The **Bull Terrier**'s loyalty will always win,
With a loving heart and a curious mind,
This breed is a friend that's hard to find.

The **Border Terrier** is a scrappy little breed,
With a wiry coat and a body full of speed,
Its obedience and courage are beyond compare,
A true friend and companion that's always there.

The **Welsh Springer Spaniel** stands tall,
Unfailing and friendly, never letting their owners fall,
With a wag of their tail and a bark of delight,
They'll be your guide through day and night.

The **Jack Russell Terrier** is small but mighty,
With energy that's boundless and never flighty,
With a clever mind and a fearless heart,
This breed is a best friend from the start.

The **Komondor**'s coat is a sight to behold,
Long cords of hair, like ropes of gold.
A guardian dog, steadfast and true,
Loyal to their family through and through.

An **Airedale Terrier** is a breed so rare,
With bristly hair and a fun stare,
Its energy and spunk are beyond compare,
And it'll keep you laughing without a care.

A **Greyhound**, sleek and slender,
With muscles built to render,
Graceful strides, a sight to behold,
A true champion, brave and bold.

With a rich coat so fine,
An **Irish Setter**'s beauty is divine.
With eyes so bright and full of glee,
Their wagging tail brings pure ecstasy.

A **Lhasa Apso** is small and smart,
With fur so fluffy, a work of art.
A keen watchdog, alert and aware,
Their devotion and love beyond compare.

With wrinkles so deep and eyes so wide,
A **Shar Pei** stands out with fierce pride,
Their loving hearts will never subside,
A faithful friend always by your side.